How To Maintain Behavior

SECOND EDITION

Karen Esveldt-Dawson
and
Alan E. Kazdin

How To Manage Behavior Series

R. Vance Hall
and
Marilyn L. Hall
Series Editors

pro·ed
An International Publisher
8700 Shoal Creek Boulevard
Austin, Texas 78757-6897
800/897-3202 Fax 800/397-7633
Order online at http://www.proedinc.com

PENSACOLA STATE-PEN LIBRARY

© 1998 by PRO-ED, Inc.
8700 Shoal Creek Boulevard
Austin, Texas 78757-6897
800/897-3202 Fax 800/397-7633
www.proedinc.com

All rights reserved. No part of the material protected by this
copyright notice may be reproduced or used in any form or by
any means, electronic or mechanical, including photocopying,
recording, or by any information storage and retrieval system,
without the prior written permission of the copyright owner.

Library of Congress Cataloging-in-Publication Data

Esveldt-Dawson, Karen
    How to maintain behavior / Karen Esveldt-Dawson and Alan E. Kazdin.
      p.   cm.—(How to manage behavior series)
    Includes bibliographical references.
    ISBN 0-89079-763-3 (pbk.:alk. paper)
    1. Behavior modification.   I. Kazdin, Alan E.   II. Title.
   III. Series.
BF637.B4K43   1998
153.8'5—dc21   97-45710
                                                      CIP

This book is designed in Palatino and Frutiger.

Printed in the United States of America

5 6 7 8 9 10 11 12 13 14 17 16 15 14 13

Contents

Preface to Series

The first edition of the *How To Manage Behavior Series* was launched some 15 years ago in response to a perceived need for teaching aids that could be used by therapists and trainers. The widespread demand for the series has demonstrated the need by therapists and trainers for nontechnical materials for training and treatment aids for parents, teachers, and students. Publication of this revised series includes many updated titles of the original series. In addition, several new titles have been added, largely in response to therapists and trainers who have used the series. A few titles of the original series that proved to be in less demand have been replaced. We hope the new titles will increase the usefulness of the series.

The editors are indebted to Steven Mathews, Vice President of PRO-ED, who was instrumental in the production of the revised series, as was Robert K. Hoyt, Jr. of H & H Enterprises in producing the original version.

These books are designed to teach practitioners, including parents, specific behavioral procedures to use in managing the behaviors of children, students, and other persons whose behavior may be creating disruption or interference at home, at school, or on the job. The books are nontechnical, step-by-step instructional manuals that define the procedure, provide numerous examples, and allow the reader to make oral or written responses.

The exercises in these books are designed to be used under the direction of someone (usually a professional) with a background in the behavioral principles and procedures on which the techniques are based.

The booklets in the series are similar in format but are flexible enough to be adapted to a number of different teaching situations and training environments.

R. Vance Hall, PhD, is Senior Scientist Emeritus of The Bureau of Child Research and Professor Emeritus of Human Development and Family Life and Special Education at the University of Kansas. He was a pioneer in carrying out behavioral research in classrooms and in homes. Marilyn L. Hall, EdD, taught and carried out research in regular and special public school classrooms. While at the University of Kansas, she developed programs for training parents to use systematic behavior change procedures and was a successful behavior therapist specializing in child management and marriage relationships.

As always, we invite your comments, suggestions, and questions. We are always happy to hear of your successes in changing your own behaviors and the behaviors of other persons to make your lives more pleasant, productive, and purposeful.

R. Vance Hall &
Marilyn L. Hall,
Series Editors

How To Manage Behavior Series

How To Maintain Behavior

How To Motivate Others Through Feedback

How To Negotiate a Behavioral Contract

How To Select Reinforcers

How To Teach Social Skills

How To Teach Through Modeling and Imitation

How To Use Group Contingencies

How To Use Planned Ignoring

How To Use Prompts To Initiate Behavior

How To Use Response Cost

How To Use Systematic Attention and Approval

How To Use Time-Out

Introduction

This manual provides information about how to maintain behavior after a behavior modification program is withdrawn. Several behavioral techniques have been devised to develop desired behaviors and eliminate undesired behaviors among children and adults. Techniques such as systematic attention and approval, planned ignoring, feedback, modeling positive practice, and others are described in other manuals in this series. These techniques are very effective in developing desired behaviors in classroom, home, institutional, and community settings.

After behavior is developed, the management techniques are withdrawn so the client can function under ordinary living conditions. When a program is terminated, however, behavior often returns to its original level before the behavioral procedure was applied. Gains are likely to be lost unless the termination of the program is planned and special procedures are introduced to maintain the new behavior.

This manual presents various methods that can be used alone or in combination to maintain behavior. The techniques are designed to be implemented after behavior changes have been achieved and before the program is completely withdrawn. The manual presents different techniques to maintain behavior and illustrates their applications with different clients, behaviors, and settings. Exercises are provided to help you develop skill in applying the different procedures.

Maintenance of Behavior

Maintenance of behavior refers to a process used to ensure that either the increases in appropriate responses or the decreases in inappropriate responses

Karen Esveldt-Dawson, MA, is a behavior therapist in private practice for children and adults, and teaches a graduate course in behavior therapy at Humbolt State University. She formerly was a research administrator and specialty counselor at the University of Pittsburgh School of Medicine, Division of Child and Adolescent Psychiatry, and at the Western Psychiatric Institute and Clinic. She has also been a teacher/team leader at the elementary level and a training/research coordinator at the University of California at Los Angeles in the Neuropsychiatric Institute of the Department of Psychiatry. Esveldt-Dawson has taught classes at the University of Washington, the University of Pittsburgh, and the University of California at Los Angeles.

Alan E. Kazdin, PhD, is Professor and Chairman of Psychology at Yale University, Professor in the Child Study Center (Child Psychiatry), and Director of the Yale Child Conduct Clinic, an outpatient treatment service for children and their families. His research focuses primarily on child, parent, family, and contextual influences on aggressive and antisocial behavior in children and adolescents and the effectiveness of child psychotherapy. His writings include the book *Behavior Modification in Applied Settings* (5th ed., Brooks/Cole) which elaborates behavior-change principles and techniques that are applied at home, at school, and in the community at large.

will last. When the desired level of behavior is reached, one should concentrate on how to maintain this behavior at an acceptable level. Although special reinforcement, reductive, or extinction techniques may be very successful in changing behavior, the ultimate success of the program depends on whether the gains are sustained when the techniques are no longer in effect. The importance of maintenance in different settings is illustrated in the cases described below.

At Home

Brian and Gayleen are concerned about their 7-year-old daughter Mary. Since her baby brother Rick was born about 10 months ago, Mary has become increasingly unmanageable. When Brian or Gayleen attends to the baby, Mary begins to cry and whine, and continues this until they stop attending to the baby.

Brian and Gayleen decide to pay more attention to her when she does not whine and cry, and to give less attention to her when she does. They explain to Mary that she will earn a point when they are with the baby if she waits quietly or entertains herself. When she saves 4 points, she will have 10 minutes of undivided attention from either her mom or her dad to play a short game or do a puzzle.

As the program continues, Brian and Gayleen notice that Mary cries and whines much less frequently. They reward Mary every time she does not whine when they are with the baby. After about 2 weeks, Mary's crying and whining disappear. Brian and Gayleen are very pleased but they do not want to continue with the point program forever.

They also feel that Mary should be given more responsibility. They tell Mary that because she has been doing so well, she may help with the baby if she wants (i.e., change his diaper, help feed and play with him). They also tell her that each night she may have a special time with either her mother or her father. The parents make an effort to have more of Mary's friends over so that she has things she wants to do. They continue to keep track of the amount of whining and crying and are very satisfied when it does not increase after they drop the special point program.

What was the parents' reinforcement program designed to do? _____

_____

_____

Was Mary's behavior maintained? _____

(continues)

Discuss why you think the behavior was or was not maintained. _____

_____

_____

At School

Tyson is a 7-year-old second grader at the neighborhood elementary school. The teachers informed Tyson's parents that he had been destroying the other children's books. This, of course, was of great concern to his parents. Therefore, a parent–teacher conference was set up. It was decided that when Tyson destroys other children's books, he will sit in the hall for 5 minutes. Also, a chart was made for recording his behavior. Each day that Tyson does not destroy any of the other children's books, he receives a star on his chart. During the first week, Tyson did fairly well. This program continued for 3 more weeks and Tyson had only one incident of destroying things. Tyson was doing so well it was decided that he did not need to continue the program, so the program was stopped. But the destructive behavior has started again. Tyson's parents and teacher are very concerned. Another conference has been scheduled so a decision can be made on what to do next.

What was the program designed to do? _____

_____

_____

Did it work? _____

Was Tyson's behavior maintained? _____

Discuss why you think the behavior was or was not maintained. _____

_____

_____

In a Residential Setting

Danny is an 8-year-old severely retarded boy who has been in an institution for the past 2 years. Among his problems is severe aggressive behavior. Specifically, he bites himself on the arm and hand and frequently bites other children and staff members. One of the staff members, who has primary responsibility for his care, designs a program based on reinforcement and overcorrection. For every 10 minutes he goes without biting himself or someone else, Danny earns a small piece of cereal. A timer is used to help monitor the time. When he does bite himself, he is put through an overcorrection procedure in which he must move his head back and forth and to the side 10 times. This procedure provides behaviors that compete with the undesired head movements associated with biting.

After about 3 weeks, Danny's biting behavior is reduced significantly. The staff decides that the behavior is low enough that there is no need for the program. So both the reinforcement and overcorrection procedures are withdrawn. The behavior remains low for the first few days, but for no clear reason, Danny then begins biting himself and others again. Within a week, the behavior returns to its original level.

What was the program designed to do? _____

_____

Did it work? _____

Did Danny's behavior improve? _____

Discuss why you think it was or was not maintained. _____

_____

_____

_____

The above illustrations are from programs that increased desirable behavior or decreased undesirable behaviors. In each case, the programs were effective. The major differences among the programs were in how well the gains were maintained when the programs were no longer in effect. Gains often are not maintained unless special procedures are implemented specifically for maintenance. This manual presents several methods that can be used to maintain behavior.

By now you probably have an idea of what is meant by maintaining behavior. In your own words, describe what **maintaining behavior** means to you.

_____

_____

_____

_____

You were correct if you said something similar to the following: Maintaining behavior means that the gains made in changing some behavior will last when the program is withdrawn.

Describe a situation you are familiar with where a behavior modification program was successful and the behavior was maintained.

_____

_____

_____

_____

Why do you feel the behavior was maintained?

_____

_____

_____

_____

(*continues*)

Now describe a situation you are familiar with where the program was successful but the behavior was not maintained.

_____

_____

_____

_____

_____

_____

Why was the behavior not maintained? _____

_____

_____

_____

Basic Procedures To Maintain Behavior

To begin maintenance procedures, the behavior must be at an acceptable level. If the behavior is not at an acceptable level, the program needs to be changed. Once satisfactory changes have been achieved, it is appropriate to consider how to maintain these gains. Six different techniques for maintaining behavior are described and illustrated below. Although the techniques are discussed individually, they may be combined to maximize the chances that the behaviors will be maintained at the high level achieved while the behavioral program was in effect (Foxx, Faw, & Weber, 1991).

Intermittent Reinforcement

When behavior is being developed, reinforcement may be given every time the behavior occurs. Gradually, the behavior can be rewarded less often until reinforcement is provided infrequently or not at all.

Behavior develops more rapidly and occurs more often if it is reinforced each time it occurs. When reinforcement is given after each occurrence of the desired behavior, this is continuous reinforcement.

After behavior has developed at a high rate, it does not have to be reinforced every time. The reinforcer can be given intermittently so some performances of the desired responses are rewarded but others are not. When reinforcement is given only after some occurrences of the behavior, this is intermittent reinforcement. Intermittent reinforcement is effective in maintaining behavior (Baer, Blount, Detrick, & Stokes, 1987).

A teacher may praise a child for raising his or her hand to ask permission for something. At first, praise may be given each time the child performs this behavior. When behavior is at a high level, the teacher can reinforce the behavior most, but not all, of the time. To maintain behavior it can be reinforced on fewer and fewer occasions. Over time, the reinforcer comes perhaps for every 5th occurrence, then for every 10th or 20th occurrence. Praise soon may be given on few or no occasions after the behavior occurs, but the behavior is still maintained at a high level.

The crucial elements to remember when using intermittent reinforcement are to

1. Reinforce fewer and fewer occurrences of the desired behavior.

2. Proceed gradually so the change from continuous to highly intermittent reinforcement is not abrupt (e.g., every 2nd, 5th, 10th, 15th response).

The following example shows the correct use of intermittent reinforcement to maintain desired behavior.

Matt, who is 8 years old, and Jenny, who is 6 years old, are always fighting. Mrs. Potter knows that all brothers and sisters fight once in a while but Matt and Jenny seem to argue and fight from the minute they get home from school until bedtime. To remedy the problem, Mrs. Potter decides to praise the children each time they interact appropriately. During the first 2 weeks, Mrs. Potter is very careful to be sure that each time the children are interacting appropriately she walks over and tells them how nice it is to see them playing together, hugs each child, and offers a small snack as a reward. She is careful to vary what she says or does so the children do not get bored with her attention. Also, she makes sure each time the children know why they are being reinforced.

By the end of the second week, the children spend almost all their time together interacting appropriately. At this point Mrs. Potter decides to begin moving from reinforcing every occurrence of the desired behavior (continuous reinforcement) to reinforcing each 2 or 3 occurrences, and then every 4 or 5 occurrences, and so on. As Mrs. Potter reinforces fewer and fewer occurrences of appropriate play, she is careful to make sure that the rate of appropriate play is maintained. Eventually Mrs. Potter rarely goes to the children with the sole purpose of rewarding their appropriate interactions, yet appropriate interactions continue at a very high level.

Describe in your own words what **intermittent reinforcement** as a maintenance procedure means.

_____

_____

What are the crucial points to remember in using intermittent reinforcement to maintain behavior?

1. _____

2. _____

If your answer calls for reinforcing fewer and fewer occurrences of the desired behavior, and says that reducing reinforcement should be gradual, you are doing a great job!

The reinforcement program described next has been successful and is ready for the maintenance phase. Read the description and describe how you would use intermittent reinforcement to achieve maintenance.

Bang! The screen door slams again and Zachary, 5, enters the kitchen. His mother yells, "Please don't slam that door. I've told you a hundred times not to slam the door." That night Zachary's mother decides to try a new program to help Zachary remember to close the screen door quietly. She tells him that every time he closes the door quietly, he will get a sticker. It has been 2 weeks now, and Zachary has done beautifully. He rarely slams the door and continuous reinforcement is no longer needed.

Describe your plan for achieving maintenance. _____

_____

_____

Delayed Reinforcement

When a reinforcement program is begun, it is essential to provide consequences immediately after the desired behavior occurs. The more immediate the reinforcer, the better the effects. In the beginning of a program, when the desired behavior may not occur very often, immediate reinforcement is especially important. After behavior develops and is performed consistently, presentation of the reinforcer can be delayed.

Behavior can be maintained by gradually increasing the delay between the desired behavior and reinforcement. Early in the program, reinforcement is provided immediately after the behavior occurs. When behavior changes, a relatively brief delay is introduced. The delay between the behavior and the reinforcement can be increased gradually without a loss of the behavior. Eventually the reinforcement can be terminated because the person learns to perform the response without direct reinforcement (Dunlap, Koegel, Johnson, & O'Neill, 1987).

For example, to improve table manners at home, parents may provide children with reinforcers such as stars for eating with utensils instead of their fingers, not talking with their mouths full, and asking for food to be passed rather than standing up and reaching across the table. The stars can be exchanged for dimes after the meal. When the program begins, the stars should be given immediately after the child performs a desired behavior. During the meal itself, the parents may paste a star on a card or simply pass a star to the child. As the desired behaviors develop, the delay between the responses and the stars is increased. First the delay may begin by giving the stars at the end of the meal. After the meal is finished, the parents give the children their stars and the dimes that go with them. The reinforcers can be delayed further by waiting until the end of the day and providing all of the stars for each meal the child ate at home on that day. Longer delays occur between the correct eating behavior and receiving the stars, until earnings are given at the end of each week.

An alternative way to introduce delayed reinforcement is to give the stars immediately during the meals but to increase the delay between earning the stars and exchanging them for other rewards. Early in the program, the child may exchange the stars at the end of each meal so dimes are given immediately. Over time, the delay between earning stars and exchanging them for other rewards is increased. By the end of the program, the child receives the stars but those stars are infrequently exchanged for other rewards. Behavior is then being maintained by the feedback parents provide by giving the stars and not from other rewards.

The crucial elements to remember about using delayed reinforcement are to

1. Require more and more time to pass between the behavior and getting the reward.

2. Make sure this increased delay is approached gradually.

The following example shows the correct use of delayed reinforcement to maintain desired behavior.

Moriah, a strong-willed 3-year-old, had begun to adamantly protest taking her morning bath. Beginning as a verbal complaint, her efforts to avoid the tub escalated into screaming, running away, scratching and hitting her father, and even splashing water out of the tub. Greg had tried many enticements, such as putting fun toys in the bath, warning her in advance, even getting angry with Moriah. Finally, after repeated failures, Greg decided to set up a program involving immediate reinforcement for each time Moriah complied with her bathtime. She and Greg played a rough-and-tumble tickle game for 15 minutes immediately after a successful bathtime. After 3 weeks Greg was impressed with the difference in Moriah's behavior and wanted to discontinue the program. He decided to delay the time between the bath and the rough-and-tumble game. First, the delay was only ½ hour long. Bathtime continued to go well, so he increased the time between the bath and the reward to 1 hour. Eventually he waited up to 2 or 3 hours until he played the game with her. As Greg does not want to quit spending playtime with her, he has continued to play the rough-and-tumble game with Moriah at random times in the day. He feels that Moriah has continued her good bathtime behavior without a direct connection to the reward.

Describe what **delayed reinforcement** means as a maintenance procedure.

_____

_____

_____

_____

What are the important points to remember about using delayed reinforcement?

1. _____

2. _____

You were correct if you said increasing the delay between the behavior and the reward, and increasing the delay gradually.

To give you a chance to practice your new skills in using delayed reinforcement, the program below requires a maintenance procedure. Please read it and describe your plan for maintenance using delayed reinforcement.

Mrs. Thompson decided it was time for Brittany to be toilet trained. She had been working on getting Brittany to understand the difference between wet and dry. She explained to Brittany that each time she urinated in the toilet, she would immediately receive a hug, a kiss, and a penny to use in a gumball machine. Mrs. Thompson was very careful to take Brittany to the toilet approximately every 20 minutes to see if she could go. Each time Brittany was able to go in the toilet, Mrs. Thompson immediately gave Brittany lots of praise and a penny so she could buy a piece of gum immediately. Both Brittany and Mrs. Thompson were elated with the toilet training.

Describe how you would use delayed reinforcement to achieve maintenance.

_____

_____

_____

Fading

When a behavior modification program is ended abruptly, the gains in behavior may be lost. A transition period helps withdraw the program gradually. The gradual removal of the program prepares the person for everyday situations in which he or she must function. In everyday situations, specific rewards are not provided immediately after the behaviors, as they are during a special reinforcement program. Fading refers to gradually withdrawing or phasing out the highly structured behavioral program. Using increasingly intermittent or delayed reinforcement is effective in fading a program. However, other procedures can be used to move the person toward maintenance of behavior with few or no direct contingencies needed to sustain performance.

The most commonly used technique is to divide the program into different levels (Kazdin & Mascitelli, 1980). The first level is highly structured so that very explicit contingencies specify the behaviors that must be performed to earn specific rewards. The rewards are delivered relatively often and with little delay. As the person performs the behaviors consistently, he or she advances to the next level. At this level, fewer contingencies are placed on performance so there is less of a direct connection between behaviors and immediate rewards.

For example, a classroom program may involve three levels. At the first level, children may earn points for completing their classroom assignments and turning in homework on time. The points may be given for specific assignments several times during the day and exchanged for free time and the use of games. After children perform well at the first level for a few weeks, they may advance to the next level.

At the second level, the children have access to the free time each day without having their assignments checked every time and without receiving points. The teacher may check the work once in a while or at the end of the week. Alternatively, the children may be instructed to keep their own record, which the teacher checks. The children are given free time each day as long as they maintain high levels of performance.

A third level might be one in which the children continue to have access to the available rewards but are placed in a position of responsibility where they help monitor the work of other children at different levels. By this point the children are enjoying the benefits of the rewards but are performing without direct consequences for specific behavior.

The program has been faded because the contingencies have been withdrawn.

The crucial points to remember about using the technique of gradually fading the program to maintain behavior are to

1. Gradually reduce the highly structured connection between specific behaviors and specific rewards.

2. Have distinct levels of the program. Two or three levels usually are enough.

At the first level, contingencies specify the exact behaviors to be performed before receiving a specific reward. Rewards are provided frequently and immediately. At the second level, the connection between the behavior and the reward is reduced. The rewards or privileges are made available but the behavior is checked only once in a while. At the third level, there may be little connection between specific behavior and rewards. The rewards are available and the child continues to perform at a high level while assuming more responsibility for his or her behavior. By the time persons are at the final level, they should be performing the desired behaviors largely on their own and with no immediate consequences.

The following example shows how gradual fading of the program can be appropriately applied to assist in maintenance.

Steve, having just turned 16, had received his driver's license. Now the family car was an added necessity to his weekend plans. But when he was allowed to use the car, he always came back 1 to 2 hours later than he had promised. Steve also failed to be where he said he was going to be. Mr. and Mrs. Wilson were very concerned. Steve had been such a good child but his lack of punctuality and reliability with the car were getting out of hand. Soon every time Steve asked for the car, an argument ensued. Mr. and Mrs. Wilson decided to try something new. Their idea developed into a program with three levels. Steve's access to the car was increased, along with his freedom, when he was able to show greater responsibility. Steve was told he could have the car one night on the weekend and could stay out until 11:00. He was to tell them where he would be along with the number where he could be reached. He was also told that if he was where he said he was supposed to be and not more than 10 minutes late, he would be allowed to have the car next week.

The parents were very careful to call the number he provided each time Steve had the car and to be awake when he came home. Mr. and Mrs. Wilson were very pleased with Steve's behavior. He returned on time and was where he said he would be. They felt that they could gradually fade the highly structured contingencies to help Steve assume more responsibility for his behavior. They wanted Steve ultimately to behave appropriately without such strict and constant monitoring. They decided to move to phoning only once in a while and not to be up every time he came home. Steve continued to do well. The final level was to require only a statement of where he was going, trusting him to be home on time. Steve was also given the car more often because of his consistently good behavior. Moving slowly from a very closely controlled program to a program in which Steve assumed more responsibility provided an excellent solution to a situation that had been very unpleasant.

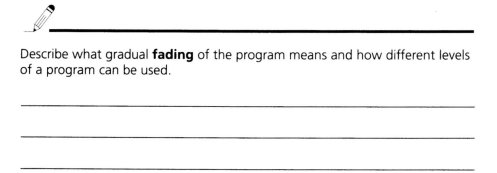

Describe what gradual **fading** of the program means and how different levels of a program can be used.

_____

_____

_____

Your answer should include a statement about slowly reducing the connection between certain behaviors and their rewards. The first level should be described as one where specific behaviors result in specific rewards. The second level involves continued use of the rewards but checking behavior less frequently. The final level involves much more independent functioning with little external control.

A situation is described below in which gradual fading of the program is needed to maintain behavior.

Coach Benson was upset again over his football team's mediocre performance Saturday afternoon. They had forgotten plays, made errors, and shown little enthusiasm throughout the game. After a heated team meeting, the coach announced that henceforth practices would be run differently. Under the direct supervision of the coach, all players were to run 10 laps before and after practice, do 15 wind sprints to conclude the day, and practice each play five times daily. A chart was made for each player and was checked off by the coach each day. Any player failing to accomplish all of the requirements was not allowed to play in that week's game.

Describe how you would use gradual fading of the program for this situation.

Shifting from Contrived to Naturally Occurring Reinforcers

Naturally occurring reinforcers refer to consequences normally present or available. These include praise and attention from others, privileges, and activities such as recess, free time, or access to games that are part of classroom or home routines. Another book in this series discusses several naturally occurring reinforcers that may be used in a behavioral program (*How To Select Reinforcers*, Hall & Hall, 1998a.)

Some rewards are called *contrived reinforcers* because they are not usually available in the setting or are not usually provided for the behaviors in the program. For example, candy may be given to children for playing nicely with brothers and sisters or for doing chores, or points and tokens may be given to children with mental retardation in a special classroom to help them learn academic tasks. In everyday life, candy and tokens are not provided for these behaviors, but such rewards may be extremely useful when developing performance. Later, when behavior is to be maintained, it is important to shift from contrived to more naturally occurring reinforcers. When rewards are shifted to naturally occurring reinforcers, it is easier to maintain performance (Kallman, Hersen, & O'Toole, 1975).

For example, a teacher of a special class of high school students may wish to increase the completion of homework. Candy, small prizes, and the opportunity to earn a compact disc (through a class lottery) may be offered to the students. Because candy and prizes do not ordinarily follow academic performance, the teacher should begin to substitute more naturally occurring reinforcers after the students complete their assignments on a regular basis.

Instead of candy and prizes, the teacher may emphasize praise and attention. The teacher may make a list of students who complete their work and publicly display the list so that excellent performance is conspicuous. The school principal should be enlisted to stop by occasionally to make a note of who is on the list and to congratulate these students in front of the other members of the class. Such approval is normally not available but represents a transition from contrived tangible rewards, such as candy and prizes, to more naturally occurring rewards, such as teacher and peer praise.

The important element to remember about this procedure is to move from giving rewards that are artificial to rewards that occur naturally as part of the daily routine.

An example of shifting from contrived to naturally occurring reinforcers follows.

"Ross, come to bed now! I've asked you four times already. Come on, you're already 20 minutes past your bedtime!" Mrs. Twitchell was growing more and more upset by Ross' dismissal of her request to go to bed. The routine of struggling to get Ross to go to bed had become unbearable. Mrs. Twitchell decided to start a system of rewards for Ross when he went to bed within 10 minutes of his bedtime. Each smooth bedtime that Ross performed resulted in a small trinket being given to him that night. After a few weeks of this program, Ross' bedtimes had become decidedly more pleasant for both him and his mother. Ross had even begun getting ready for bed before being asked by his mother. Wanting to reward Ross with a more natural reinforcer, consequence, or reward, Mrs. Twitchell decided to give Ross either a longer reading time or the chance to play with his video game for a longer period the next day. Both of these rewards were naturally available in his environment. Ross was motivated by his ability to play longer with his video games so he continued to go to bed on time and without complaint.

How would you describe the procedure of shifting from contrived to naturally occurring reinforcers?

_____

_____

(continues)

You are showing excellent comprehension if your answer was something like the following: Shifting from contrived to naturally occurring reinforcers means starting the program with artificial rewards, such as candy or toys, and then switching to rewards that are normally available, such as attention, praise, and activities, once the desired behavior has been achieved.

A program using contrived rewards is described below. Please read it and then write your plan for shifting to naturally occurring reinforcers.

Mr. Chan, director of a weight loss clinic for children, had for many years conducted group therapy in which children talked about their overeating and the reasons for not losing weight. He began to pursue a new approach that might have more direct impact on the children's weight losses. Children were individually placed on exercise and calorie regimens where they could earn points and prizes for adhering to their individual programs. The clinic wished to encourage the use of naturally occurring reinforcers to ensure continuation of the regimen in everyday lives.

Please describe how you would shift to more natural reinforcers.

_____

_____

_____

Developing Peer Support

Attention and approval from peers are powerful reinforcers. Peer support is a rich source of influence in changing behavior and maintaining changes. Peer attention and approval are natural reinforcers and are part of shifting from contrived to naturally occurring reinforcers, as discussed above. Peer support warrants additional mention because of the range of options it provides for maintaining behavior.

When a program has developed the desired behavior, the situation can be restructured so peers provide direct reinforcing consequences to the person who is the focus of the program. One way to encourage peer reinforcement is to have peers share the rewarding consequences. For example, a child may earn special privileges for appropriate classroom behavior. The reward may also be provided to the child's peers even though they did not earn it with their own behavior. When persons earn consequences for others as well as for themselves, this alters the reactions of peers. Peers begin to support and encourage appropriate behaviors of the target child because that behavior earns rewards for them. Peer support becomes a major influence that continues after the specific contingencies are withdrawn.

Peer support can be developed by having peers directly administer rewarding consequences to the target child. For example, in the home an older brother or sister can provide direct consequences (praise, attention, stars, participation in games) to a younger sibling. With the aid of the parents, the older sibling can give rewards for the desired behaviors. To make sure that the older sibling performs this task well, he or she may receive rewards directly from the parents. Direct reinforcement from one sibling to another can be very effective. Also, when the program has ended, behavior is likely to be maintained because the behavior in the home is under the influence of the older sibling (Lancioni, 1982).

Occasionally, peer support for a target behavior can be incorporated into a program as part of the shift from contrived to naturally occurring reinforcers. For example, a program may at first depend upon prizes, snacks, and special activities as reinforcers. As behavior improves, more naturally occurring peer reinforcers may be included. Children who earn a special reward may be asked to come before classmates to receive applause or even a standing ovation, or the reward may be to serve as a class captain or leader for a day with special privileges that may be accorded that position.

The crucial ingredient to remember about using peer support as a technique for maintenance is that the peers must take an active part in the target child's program. This can be accomplished by having the peers enjoy the rewards earned or by having the peers actually monitor behavior and dispense the rewards.

The following example illustrates the use of peer support in a maintenance program.

Tessa, who was in the fourth grade, had become the class clown. Whenever she had the chance, she would talk out in class, make jokes, throw paper airplanes across the room, and generally disrupt the entire class. The teacher could not control Tessa and decided to try a new program. He told Tessa that for every half hour she was attentive and appropriate she would earn a checkmark. At the end of the day, she would need five checkmarks to get a "good worker award" from the teacher. For 2 weeks the program seemed to work well. Tessa was quite good as long as the teacher was in the room. Whenever he was not there, Tessa was back to her old tricks. On the playground, in the lunchroom, and in other places where the teacher was not present, Tessa's behavior was still very disruptive. A problem also arose when the teacher tried to fade his involvement in the class program. When he tried to increase the time period between the behavior and the delivery of the checkmarks, Tessa started to become more and more disruptive. At this point the teacher decided that Tessa's good behavior was not being maintained in the classroom and that it had not maintained or carried over to other situations where he was not present. He enlisted the help of Tessa's peers to monitor and reinforce appropriate behavior. Instead of the teacher checking on Tessa's behavior, her classmates helped decide when she should receive a checkmark. The teacher continued to monitor the peers to make sure they were correctly assessing Tessa's behavior. The peers also took turns designing and making up Tessa's "good worker certificate." Tessa was extremely pleased to have her friends help her. Her behavior improved in other situations even though no direct rewards were given outside the classroom. On the playground and in the cafeteria, teachers reported that peers helped remind Tessa. Even when the program was slowly faded and discontinued, the teacher reported that Tessa's behavior continued to improve and that occasionally he overheard a peer praising appropriate behavior or reminding Tessa to behave.

Describe what **developing peer support** means. _____

_____

_____

_____

_____

Your answer should include a statement about using other persons who have contact with the target person as active members of the reinforcement program.

Please read the incident described below and plan a maintenance program that uses peer support.

Noah, who just started second grade, was a very shy child. He isolated himself on the playground and never played with the other children. Mrs. Roe, his teacher, decided to start a reinforcement program to help Noah play with other children. Noah was told that whenever he was playing with another child, Mrs. Roe would give him a checkmark on a card she carried. At the end of recess, Noah could exchange the checkmarks for a prize.

_____

Describe your program to develop peer support. _____

_____

_____

_____

Maintaining Behaviors in New Situations

The procedures discussed above can be used to maintain behaviors in the environments where reinforcement was given. In addition to maintenance of behavior, a child is likely to enter new situations where the program has never been in effect. For example, a delinquent youth may be released from an institution or group home where a behavioral program was in effect. Newly learned behaviors not only need to be maintained after the program has been terminated but also must be extended to the new situation.

When behavioral programs are implemented in only one setting, behaviors may not carry over to new settings. For example, if behavior improves at school, the changes may not carry over to the home. Similarly, if behavior is altered by a program in a classroom, the changes may not carry over to classes the child attends during other hours of the day.

To develop and maintain behaviors in new situations, it is important to extend the reinforcement program to the new settings. For example, although reinforcement may increase the social interaction of a withdrawn child while he or she plays at recess in school, the child's increased social behavior may not carry over to play at home. To extend behavior to the home, the parents need to reinforce the desired behaviors. There may be many other situations (e.g., parties, vacations) where parents and teachers can increase social behavior. Not all these situations need special reinforcement programs. If behavior is rewarded systematically in several new situations, it is likely to extend to novel situations and be maintained after the program has been terminated (Rasing & Duker, 1992).

In some instances, a reinforcement program may be carried out by only one person, such as a parent, teacher, or staff member. If the target behaviors are to be performed and maintained in the presence of other persons, reinforcement needs to be administered by those other persons. For example, a child with mental retardation in an institution may show the desired behaviors in the presence of the staff member who has consistently provided reinforcement, but not in the presence of other staff members. Those other staff members need to be included in the program. If those persons provide reinforcing consequences, behavior not only will be performed in their presence but will transfer to persons who have not been associated with reinforcement. Also, if behavior is developed by a variety of staff members and situations, it is more likely to be maintained.

In general, when the goal is to maintain behavior in different situations, or in the presence of different persons, it is important to extend the program to those situations and persons. When behavior is rewarded under different stimuli, it is more likely to generalize to new situations and to be maintained. With the involvement of a variety of situations and trainers, the child demonstrates the behavior changes more consistently and is less likely to revert after a program has ended.

The important thing to remember about maintaining behaviors in new situations is the need to extend the reinforcement program to the new setting and to include other persons in the administration of the program.

The following example illustrates the successful application of procedures for the maintenance of a behavior in new situations.

Mark, a 17-year-old high school student, was admitted to the County Drug Clinic, a live-in program for adolescents with severe drug problems. During the initial month Mark was not allowed to leave the clinic. He was also put on a strict behavioral program with monetary rewards for drug-free days and productive daily activities. Because many persons return to drugs after leaving the treatment facility, the program involved parent participation to help maintain the changes when the residents returned home. Parents visited the treatment facility often and were trained to continue the behavioral program at home. In the second month Mark was permitted overnight visits at home. While at home his parents continued the behavioral programs employing the same rewards the clinic had used. After 3 months Mark was home again full time, attending school and having no further problems with drugs.

What are the crucial points to remember about **maintaining behaviors in new situations?**

_____

_____

_____

You should have answered *extending the reinforcement program to the new setting and including others in the administration of the reinforcement.*

The program described next was successful in altering behavior in one particular setting. Read the description and then describe how you would achieve maintenance in new settings.

Sally, a third-grade student, had refused to speak at school, to either classmates or teachers. After determining that neither neurological nor medical problems existed that could account for her not speaking, a behavioral program was started. In a small room for 1 hour each day, a therapist worked with Sally. Each time Sally was successful in imitating what the therapist said, she received a token that she could use at the end of the hour to purchase a prize.

After 4 weeks Sally was speaking to the therapist but only while they were in the therapy room and only when they were alone. The therapist had approached Sally outside of the therapy room but Sally refused to speak to her. Also, the therapist had brought another child into the therapy room but Sally again refused to talk. It was apparent that Sally's behavior was not being maintained in a new setting or with other people.

Describe your plan for maintaining behaviors in new settings. _____

_____

_____

_____

Maintenance Guidelines

It is important to follow several guidelines as a checklist to determine whether you and the person for whom the program has been designed are ready to begin procedures to develop maintenance of behavior.

☐ 1. Be sure that the desired behavior is at the level you want.

☐ 2. Make sure you have decided upon acceptable limits for the desired behavior. This means that you should set the rate or level within which the behavior can vary during maintenance and still be acceptable.

☐ 3. Make sure you explain the changes you are making in the program before implementing them.

☐ 4. Be sure that changes in the program are not too large or too abrupt. Most program changes should be gradual.

☐ 5. Be sure to continue to monitor what happens to the desired behavior as you move to the maintenance phase.

☐ 6. Continue to use social reinforcement and praise for appropriate behavior. You may reduce the level, but some form of social praise or reinforcement should always be continued even if it is infrequent.

☐ 7. If the desired behavior is not being maintained, it is important to first return the behavior to an acceptable level before trying a different maintenance procedure.

Troubleshooting: Checking To See If Behaviors Are Maintained

The procedures for maintaining behavior assume that behaviors have been developed to a satisfactory level with a particular intervention. When the desired level of performance has been achieved, special procedures maintain behavior. Because there is no guarantee in any given instance that behaviors will be maintained, it is very important to monitor behavior carefully while the maintenance procedures are in effect and after the program has been completely withdrawn.

Measuring Behavior

The maintenance procedures all require withdrawing the program. The purpose is to remove the program while maintaining high levels of the desirable behavior. Information is needed to ensure that the improvements are not lost. Behavior must be measured to see that it is maintained. Different methods of observing behavior may be used.

One of the most convenient methods is to keep a tally or frequency count of behavior (e.g., the number of times someone gets into a fight, says something nice to others, or volunteers to participate in a class discussion). Alternatively, there may be limited opportunities to perform a particular behavior. The measure then may be the percentage of times the person completes the behavior among the available opportunities (e.g., the percentage of instances that the person complies with instructions, returns from recess or break on time, or the percentage of problems completed correctly). Finally, timing how long the behavior lasts may be a convenient measure to assess such behaviors as engaging in tantrums, getting dressed, or studying.

Other books in this series discuss methods of measuring behavior. (See *How To Use Planned Ignoring,* by Hall and Hall, 1998b, and *How To Use Systematic Attention and Approval,* by Hall & Hall, 1998c).

Charting Behavior

When evaluating the effects of maintenance procedures, it is useful to graph or chart behavior. A graph quickly shows whether behavior is maintaining its original level, even though the program is being withdrawn. For example, parents may devise a program to improve the way their child keeps his or her room. Clothing, toys, and shoes may always be out of place. Each day the parents may simply check the bed, the floor, the dresser, the nightstand, and the top of the toy chest. Each area is scored as neat (no clothing or other objects inappropriately on it) or messy.

The baseline period refers to the observations before the program is begun and is needed to measure the severity of the problem. The intervention period refers to those observations made when the program is in effect. Reinforcement for picking up clothing might be used to increase room-cleaning behavior. After behavior improves, procedures to maintain behavior can be implemented. Assume that increasing the delay between the desired behavior and delivering rewards is used to maintain behavior. The following graph shows the behavior in the baseline, intervention, and maintenance periods.

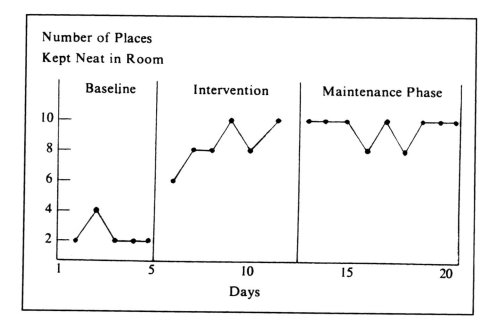

The graph shows that the child was not very neat in baseline, but that the reinforcement program improved behavior. In the final period or maintenance phase, reinforcement was delayed but the behavior was not lost. At the end of the maintenance phase, the program was completely withdrawn and behavior remained at a high level. The measurement of behavior during the maintenance period shows whether or not the original gains are lost.

What If Behavior Is Not Maintained?

The graph may show that behavior is not maintained during the maintenance phase. What should you do? The first step is to reinstate the behavior to its previously high level. This may mean temporarily returning to the original program or to a variation of it. Behavior is usually reestablished within a day or two.

After behavior returns to its high rate, maintenance procedures are again implemented. Precisely what is implemented to maintain behavior may depend upon what was tried before. If intermittent or delayed reinforcement was used, a very gradual shift should be made from continuous to intermittent or from immediate to delayed reinforcement. Behavioral gains can be lost if you proceed too rapidly in fading the reinforcement. When changes are made in the reinforcement, it is important to be sure that behavior is maintained at a high and stable level before shifting to more intermittent or delayed reinforcement.

Another option when one of the maintenance procedures does not work on the first attempt is to combine different procedures. For example, rather than using intermittent or delayed reinforcement or shifting to naturally occurring reinforcers, these different procedures can be combined. The general rule to be followed is that behavior should be maintained at a high level before withdrawing the program. The measure of how well the behavior maintains provides information for deciding whether the next step in the maintenance procedures can be taken. If behavior is maintained consistently, another change in the schedule should be tried, or the reinforcers should be changed toward more naturally occurring events.

Below is an exercise designed to give you a chance to troubleshoot and develop a successful maintenance plan:

Ben, a 12-year-old diabetic, was having problems taking his twice-daily shot of insulin. His parents found it a chore every time he needed to inject himself. He would avoid them, argue, act sullen, and sometimes go long overdue before they were able to convince him to take the needed medication. Fearing medical repercussions, his parents decided to set up a program rewarding his instant compliance with taking his medication. Each time Ben took his medication without a hassle, he would receive a check mark on a chart. After two checks he was allowed 15 minutes on the family computer for Internet use, one of Ben's favorite activities. Quickly Ben became happy to take his medication and his parents felt that he should begin to take responsibility for his own medication. They decided to delay his reinforcement. If Ben appropriately took his shots for 2 weeks, he would be allowed 15 minutes of Internet time. But within 2 weeks, Ben was once again refusing to take his medication. His parents were at a loss.

Describe two different procedures that might rectify the situation.

1. _____

2. _____

Planning Your Own Maintenance Program

Various maintenance procedures have been described. It is important that you begin to apply what you have learned. Describe a program you have used or are planning to use to increase or decrease a behavior.

_____

_____

_____

How and when did you decide you were ready for the maintenance phase?

_____

_____

_____

_____

(continues)

Describe your plans for maintaining behavior, including the specific procedures you will use.

_____

_____

_____

How and when did you inform the person of the changes in the program?

_____

_____

_____

How did you continue to monitor the behavior? _____

_____

_____

_____

Was your maintenance program successful? _____

_____

_____

_____

If not, what problems did you encounter and what maintenance program changes did you make (or what changes could you have made)?

_____

_____

_____

References and Further Reading

Albin, R. W., Horner, R. H., Koegel, R. L., & Dunlap, G. (Eds.). (1987). *Extending competent performance: Applied research on generalization and maintenance.* Eugene: University of Oregon.

Allen, J. S., Jr., Tarnowski, K. J., Simonian, S. J., Elliott, D., & Drabman, R. S. (1991). The generalization map revisited: Assessment of generalized treatment effects in child and adolescent behavior therapy. *Behavior Therapy, 23,* 393–405.

Baer, R. A., Blount, R. L., Detrick, R., & Stokes, T. F. (1987). Using intermittent reinforcement to program maintenance of verbal/nonverbal correspondence. *Journal of Applied Behavior Analysis, 20,* 179–184.

Dunlap, G., Koegel, R. L., Johnson, J., & O'Neill, R. E. (1987). Maintaining performance of autistic clients in community settings with delayed contingencies. *Journal of Applied Behavior Analysis, 20,* 179–184.

Foxx, R. M., Faw, G. D., & Weber, G. (1991). Producing generalization of inpatient adolescents' social skills with significant adults in a natural environment. *Behavioral Therapy, 22,* 85–99.

Hall, R. V., & Hall, M. L. (1998a). *How to select reinforcers.* Austin, TX: PRO-ED.

Hall, R. V., & Hall, M. L. (1998b). *How to use planned ignoring (extinction).* Austin, TX: PRO-ED.

Hall, R. V., & Hall, M. L. (1998c). *How to use systematic attention and approval.* Austin, TX: PRO-ED.

Horner, R. H., Dunlap, G., & Koegel, R. L. (Eds.). (1988). *Generalization and maintenance: Life-style changes in applied settings.* Baltimore: Brookes.

Kallman, W. H., Hersen, M., & O'Toole, D. H. The use of social reinforcement in a case of conversion reaction. *Behavior Therapy, 6,* 411–413.

Kazdin, A. E. (1994). *Behavior modification in applied settings* (5th ed.). Pacific Grove, CA: Brooks/Cole.

Kazdin, A. E., & Mascitelli, S. (1980). The opportunity to earn oneself off a token system as a reinforcer for attentive behavior. *Behavior Therapy, 11,* 68–78.

Kazdin, A. E., & Poister, R. (1973). Intermittent token reinforcement and response maintenance in extinction. *Behavior Therapy, 4,* 386–391.

Lancioni, G. E. (1982). Normal children as tutors to teach social responses to withdrawn mentally retarded schoolmates: Training, maintenance, and generalization. *Journal of Applied Behavior Analysis, 15,* 17–40.

Matson, J. S., Esveldt-Dawson, K., & O'Donnell, D. (1980). Overcorrection, modeling and reinforcement procedures for reinstating speech in a mute boy. *Child Behavior Therapy, 1,* 363–371.

Rasing, E. J., & Duker, P. C. (1992). Effects of a multifaceted training procedure on acquisition and generalization of social behaviors in language-disabled deaf children. *Journal of Applied Behavior Analysis, 25,* 723–734.

Rosen, H. S., & Rosen, L. A. (1983). Eliminating stealing: Use of stimulus control with an elementary student. *Behavior Modification, 7,* 56–63.

Stokes, T. F., & Osnes, P. G. (1989). An operant pursuit of generalization. *Behavior Therapy, 20,* 337–355.

Sullivan, M. A., & O'Leary, S. G. (1990). Maintenance following reward and cost token programs. *Behavior Therapy, 21,* 131–149.

Notes

Notes

_____

_____

_____

_____

_____

_____

_____

_____

_____

_____

_____

_____

_____

_____

_____

_____

_____

_____

_____

_____

_____

Notes

Notes

Notes

Notes

Notes